ORCA
FOOTPRINTS

Brilliant!

SHINING A LIGHT ON SUSTAINABLE ENERGY

MICHELLE MULDER

ORCA BOOK PUBLISHERS

Library and Archives Canada Cataloguing in Publication

Mulder, Michelle, 1976-
Brilliant! : shining a light on sustainable energy / Michelle Mulder.
(Orca footprints)

Includes bibliographical references and index.
Issued also in electronic format.
ISBN 978-1-4598-0221-6

1. Renewable energy sources--Juvenile literature. I. Title.
II. Series: Footprints (Victoria, B.C.)

TJ808.2.M85 2013   j333.79'4   c2013-901906-5

First published in the United States, 2013
Library of Congress Control Number: 2013935381

Summary: Innovative and sustainable energy sources light up
children's lives around the world.

Orca Book Publishers is dedicated to preserving the environment and has printed this book on Forest Stewardship Council® certified paper.

Orca Book Publishers gratefully acknowledges the support for its publishing programs provided by the following agencies: the Government of Canada through the Canada Book Fund and the Canada Council for the Arts, and the Province of British Columbia through the BC Arts Council and the Book Publishing Tax Credit.

Cover images by Corbis
Back cover images (top left to right): Wind For Schools Project/Billie Johnson, Henry Mulder, Solar Electric Light Fund (bottom left to right): Uncharted Play, Global Minimum Inc., Big Green Bus

Design by Teresa Bubela

ORCA BOOK PUBLISHERS
PO Box 5626, STN. B
Victoria, BC Canada
V8R 6S4

ORCA BOOK PUBLISHERS
PO Box 468
Custer, WA USA
98240-0468

www.orcabook.com
Printed and bound in Canada.

16 15 14 13 • 4 3 2 1

Almost all energy comes from the sun. And solar panels are just one of many ways to harness Earth-friendly energy.
ISTOCKPHOTO.COM

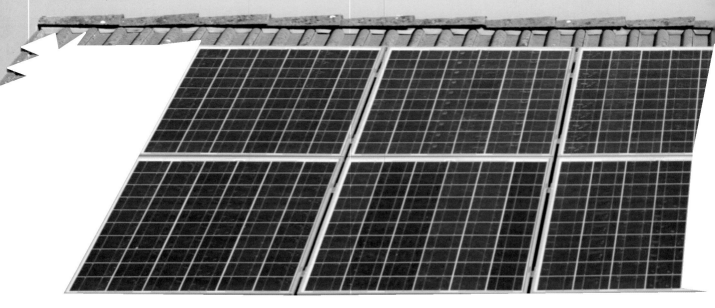

For Mo

Contents

CHAPTER ONE:
FROM SPARKS TO ZAP: THE STORY OF ENERGY

CHAPTER TWO:
WHAT MAKES IT GO?

CHAPTER THREE:
FLYING ON A FRENCH FRY!

CHAPTER FOUR:
FLICKING THE SWITCH

Introduction

I became good friends with Aracely and her family during my summer in the Dominican Republic. Their house, pictured here, was just down the hill from the school where my team lived. MICHELLE MULDER

Have you ever wondered how flicking a switch can turn on a light? How does electricity get to our houses, and where does it come from?

To be honest, I didn't wonder about this at all until I was nineteen. I spent that summer in a rural village in the Dominican Republic, helping dig ditches for a water pipeline. It was the first time I had lived in a place where none of the houses had electricity. People relied on candles and kerosene lamps for light, fire for cooking and muscle power for almost everything else. I returned to Canada thinking a lot about energy.

Soon I learned about fossil fuels and global warming. I read that people's hunger for energy—electricity for houses and fuel for cars—is harming our environment. But did you know that by avoiding fossil fuels and looking for energy in other places, people can drive cars and power their houses without harming the environment at all? In Brazil, people fuel their cars with a liquid made from leftover parts of sugarcane plants. A village in Denmark harnesses the wind to make all of its electricity. And many families in China power their stoves with gas from human and animal waste. (Yes, that's right, poop!)

So where does energy come from? Maybe you'll be as surprised as I was. Grab your Windbreaker and your sunscreen—and maybe some nose plugs—and come find out!

In this village in the Dominican Republic, the rough dirt road turned to thick mud when it rained. It wasn't generally a problem, though, because no one could afford a car. MICHELLE MULDER

Power Lines

The water pipeline that I helped dig in the Dominican Republic was powered by gravity. MICHELLE MULDER

My job in the Dominican Republic was to dig. And that's a good thing, because I didn't know anything about *designing* water pipelines. I imagined we needed a pump to get water from a lake into the pipes, and I wondered how we'd power the pump in a place without electricity. But I'd forgotten about gravity! As long as the lake at the beginning of the pipeline is higher than the field at the end, gravity will move the water. No electricity—or pumps—required. *Phew!*

CHAPTER ONE

From Sparks to Zap: The Story of Energy

LET'S HEAR IT FOR THE SUN!

Did you know that almost all energy comes from a big ball of fire in the sky? It sounds crazy, but it's true. Sure, car fuel comes from oil, and electricity comes from electricity-generating power plants. But if you live in North America, your nearest power plant likely runs on coal. Coal and the oil in car fuel are both made of tiny bacteria and plants that lived millions of years ago. And those living beings got their energy from—you guessed it!—the sun. (More about that in Chapter Two.)

But how did people learn to dig up black stuff—coal and oil—and use it for energy?

It's a long story. And it all began thousands of years ago, with fire.

Pull up a chair, grab a marshmallow and enjoy one of the first forms of energy that humans learned to master. EERIS TEIPEL

FIRE (HURRAY!)

Did you know that our ancient ancestors thought of fire as magic—a gift from the gods?

Imagine life hundreds of thousands of years ago. The sun would go down, and you'd sit around in the dark, chewing on raw meat because no one knew how to build a fire. Then one day, someone comes home with a burning stick.

(Maybe lightning struck a tree and your relative bravely "harvested" some of the flame with a stick.) Your family hurries to pile up kindling in the middle of the cave. Moments later, your home is filled with bright light and warmth, and someone cooks your steak for the first time ever!

No one knows for sure when our ancestors discovered how to control fire for their own use. Some say it was at least 400,000 years ago. A family would bring fire into a cave and keep it alive for months, or sometimes even years.

About 8,000 years ago, several groups started using fire for more than cooking and keeping warm. Someone stuck clay into a fire, where it turned into cooking pots and figurines. At least 7,000 years ago, people began using fire to melt bits of metal out of stones. Eventually, people learned to use metal to make weapons, as well as tools that were even better than stone for chopping down trees. Being able to chop down more trees in less time meant more fuel for more fires.

These days we don't worship the fire gods every time we light a candle. Instead, we recognize fire as a powerful source

Fire (or at least flame) is an important part of religious ceremonies around the world. This boy is lighting a candle at Boudanath, a Buddhist holy site in Kathmandu, Nepal. MISHA GITBERG

People have used oxen for farming and hauling heavy loads for thousands of years. This team plowed fields near Crossfield, Alberta, around 1904. GLENBOW ARCHIVES, NA-1107-5

of energy. Scientists define energy as "the ability to make things happen." For example, the energy from a campfire transforms your marshmallow into a toasty ball of gooey sweetness. The food energy from that marshmallow lets you walk to a friend's tent or jump back if you hear something rustling in the bushes. And those bushes used the energy from the sun to grow to the size they are today. Energy is all around us, getting things done.

PUT SOME MUSCLE INTO IT

Way back in those days of fire gods, people hunted their food or harvested it from the forest. Later, when they learned how to grow it themselves, they plowed the fields with tools and their own muscle power. Then someone had a big idea. An idea the size of an ox.

About 7,000 years ago, a few people in the Near East, and a few others on the Indian subcontinent, managed to tame the wild ancestors of the ox and fit them with special harnesses called *yokes*. Oxen are about seven times as powerful as humans, and the yokes allowed people to control them. Soon the beasts were plowing fields far more efficiently than humans ever could.

Later, about 4,000 to 6,000 years ago, someone figured out how to make horseshoes to protect the soft part of horses' hooves; this meant that people could ride horses without hurting them, and horses got put to work. Horseback riding allowed people to go faster and farther than ever before. Horses have even been called the world's first "rapid transit"!

Meanwhile, four-legged creatures weren't the only ones who were forced to work. Right back to the earliest times, people have used—and in some places still do use—human slaves. Huge numbers of people in early civilizations were forced to spend their entire lives hauling building materials, rowing warships, cleaning other people's houses and working in the fields.

HUFF AND PUFF

Picture yourself in ancient Egypt, standing by the Nile River with a pile of cotton sheets to sell and no way to carry them to your customers. Frustrated, you glare at the water, but then a cool breeze tickles your cheek, and you get an idea. A few days later, you're racing down the Nile in a hollowed log, using one of your cotton sheets as a sail—the world's first sailboat! No one knows exactly how sailboats were invented, but archaeologists think the first ones were built about 5,500 years ago.

About 2,700 years ago, people in Persia developed sails that they attached to buildings. The wind turned the sails of the windmill, which then turned the grindstones to grind grain. Over a thousand years later, in the fourteenth century, people of the Netherlands used windmills to pump water out of flooded land, and wind power came full circle: from being a way to get across water, to helping remove water altogether!

ENERGY FACTS: By the fourteenth century, the Dutch people saw the wind as a valuable source of energy. In fact, in 1341, a local bishop tried to legally claim that all the wind blowing through his town belonged to him, and him alone!

WATER WORKS

What do you do when the power goes off at your house? Dig in drawers for candles? Cook supper on a camp stove in the backyard? When you can't rely on the kind of energy you're used to using, you need creative thinking to get things done.

About 2,600 years ago, rich people in ancient Greece ran short of slaves to water all their crops so they began building waterwheels next to rivers. The flow of the rivers turned the wheels, which pumped water into the fields. People used this technology for thousands of years. And then, a few hundred years ago, someone figured out how to use waterwheels to make fabric!

For as long as anyone could remember, people had made fabric at home by spinning materials like sheep's wool or cotton into thread, and then weaving that thread into cloth. But at the end of the eighteenth century, businessmen in England realized that they could build factories next to rivers, the rivers could turn waterwheels, and the waterwheels could turn gears and pulleys

Power Lines

When I was growing up, my Dutch grandmother's apartment was full of windmill pictures. I was convinced that Dutch builders decorated every structure with big blades that spun in the wind, and it wasn't until years later that I realized windmills were just one of many kinds of buildings, and the blades actually use wind energy to get things done!

Me at age 9, on a family visit to Europe. HENRY MULDER

Next to a big enough river, a waterwheel like this one could help power a small mill. EERIS TEIPEL

in the mill that made the spinning and weaving machines run. People—mostly women and children—stood by to make sure the machines were running smoothly, but the main "muscle power" came from the river. Cotton mills spun more cotton than ever before, faster than ever before, and the world would never be the same again.

This was the beginning of the Industrial Revolution. As businessmen built new factories, people moved to the cities to work in those factories, where they could earn a steady wage. Factory-made cloth sold well because it was cheaper than handmade cloth. Factory owners made plenty of money, and they built more factories. All of those factories were hungry for energy, and inventors were happy to come up with new energy sources.

ENERGY FACTS: Scientists divide energy into two main types: kinetic (which means moving) or potential (which means it can be converted into kinetic energy). For example, rivers have kinetic energy. Your breakfast has potential energy—it provides the energy that you'll use throughout the day.

By the time Lewis Hine photographed this Mississippi cotton mill in 1911, cotton mills around the world were running on electricity, rather than water power. Kids as young as seven or eight worked at mills in order to help feed their families. Hine's photographs were instrumental in changing child labor laws in the United States. LIBRARY OF CONGRESS, LC-DIG-NCLC-01873

Twelfth-century monks chop down trees for firewood. BRIDGEMAN ART LIBRARY

FULL STEAM AHEAD!

Even though factories were using waterwheels for power, fire was still the main source of heat and light for most people. But they weren't using wood nearly as much anymore. For one thing, it was a lot harder to find. By the thirteenth century, people had used up so much wood that parts of Europe had run out of trees. People began to search for other energy sources, and they found a useful one deep, deep underground. Coal is a fossil fuel that comes in hard black lumps. (More about that in Chapter Two.) People loved the idea of a fuel they could buy and use right away. Coal mining became an important industry, coal miners had plenty of work, and mine owners made plenty of money. So you'd think everyone would be happy, right? Not quite. Coal mines often flooded, and coal miners drowned.

In 1698, Thomas Savery designed an engine to remove water from flooded mines. The pump worked with coal, water (steam) and pistons (metal cylinders that slide up and down inside a tube). He called his machine "The Miner's Friend." It was brilliant...except that Savery's steam pipes often burst.

In 1712, Thomas Newcomen created a more practical version. But James Watt usually gets credit for developing the first functional steam engine in 1769. His steam engine was more efficient than earlier ones, and he designed it to drive both pumps and other machines. Steam engines were just what factory owners were hoping for. Now factories could run more powerful machines, and they didn't have to be built near a river anymore. Goodbye, waterwheels! Hello, steam engines!

Hard, black lumps of energy—coal.
DAVID CANTRELL

Power Lines

When I was twenty-three, I spent a few months visiting my friend Mel, who was volunteering in Peru. She lived in a town in the mountains and often traveled to tiny settlements as part of her work. I went with her, and some of the women tried to teach me to spin wool into yarn. It looked easy: just twist the wool with your fingers and turn it onto the spool. I tried for about three minutes and managed only to tangle myself and break the wool into bits of fluff. I did do a very good job of making people laugh, though.

Spinning by hand is tougher than it looks!
MELANIE FRICOT

In 1717, Henry Beighton made an engraving to record how the Newcomen engine worked. (He couldn't take a picture because cameras hadn't been invented yet.) He called his diagram "The Engine for Raising Water with a power made by Fire."
SCIENCE AND SOCIETY PICTURE LIBRARY

Steam made a big difference in transportation too. In the early 1800s, businessmen began experimenting with steam engines on wheels. In 1830, the first passenger railroad opened in the United Kingdom. Stagecoach companies and canal owners were furious because these funny new steam-powered contraptions were putting them out of business. Other people were upset because railways seemed too dangerous. After all, trains could travel at speeds of more than twenty kilometers (twelve miles) per hour. (Imagine what they would have said about today's highways, where cars go five times that fast!) Despite all these complaints, though, *someone* must have liked the railway idea, because passenger and freight trains began to run in many countries.

Families around the world continue to use wood-burning fires for all their cooking. This woman is roasting barley for breakfast in India. MISHA GITBERG

Automobiles quickly became popular, but that didn't mean everyone could afford them. Even today, many people in the world find other ways to get from one place to the next, like these fellows in Uganda. JIM HOLMES

Henry Ford, who designed this Model T Ford car in the early 1900s, thought car fuel of the future would be made out of everything from potatoes to sawdust.
MARILYN GOULD/DREAMSTIME.COM

One of Thomas Edison's first inventions was the phonograph. This odd-looking contraption is an ancestor of our modern music-playing devices. LIBRARY OF CONGRESS, LC-DIG-CWPBH-04044

GETTING A MOVE ON

While people chugged around the countryside in steam trains, inventors were hard at work on the internal combustion engine. Instead of working with steam, these engines work with sparks and fuel.

One inventor, Rudolf Diesel, designed an engine that would run on peanut oil so that farmers could grow their own fuel. But then, in the 1850s, a new kind of fuel became more widely available: petroleum, or oil. Mr. Diesel realized it was easier and cheaper for farmers to buy petroleum than to grow enough peanuts to fill the tank. So Mr. Diesel made a few changes to his engine design and developed a petroleum fuel called—wait for it!—diesel. Other inventors made a different petroleum mixture called gasoline to use in their engines. Diesel and gasoline are still the main forms of car fuel today.

The first automobile on the market appeared in 1886. Karl Benz of Germany had put an internal combustion engine inside a metal carriage, and people loved the idea. Unlike a horse, an automobile never needed to rest. Benz's invention soon became known as the horseless carriage or motor carriage, and eventually just "car."

ELECTRIFYING

What do you get when you mix zinc, copper and a few pieces of cardboard soaked in salt water? Most of us would get a big mess, but when Alessandro Volta of Italy did this in 1800, he created the first battery that produced a reliable, steady current of electricity.

Decades later, Volta's battery would give American Thomas Edison a bright idea. What if people could use electricity, instead of candle or gas flames, to light their houses? He began to sell electric light bulbs in 1879. The bulbs were much brighter than oil and gas lamps or wax candles, but most people didn't have access to electricity to make the light bulbs work. Mr. Edison's solution? To develop the world's first electricity-generating plant!

His power plant opened in New York in 1882, and it worked in the same way that most do today. It used fuel (wood and coal) to produce heat. The heat boiled water into high-pressure steam. The steam rushed past the angled blades of a turbine, which spun around and turned a *dynamo*, a type of generator that produced electricity. Within months, electricity-generating plants popped up in other cities too.

FUELING UP

As the years went by, more people came to rely on coal and oil as fuel. Coal powered the electricity-generating plants that brought light and heat to houses. Oil fueled automobiles, planes and other kinds of engines.

Then, in the early 1900s, scientists discovered that certain underground materials, like radium and uranium, have huge amounts of energy inside them. They found a way to harness that energy, and the first nuclear power station began generating electricity in 1954. But using nuclear energy creates deadly radioactive waste.

These days, many people say it's time for a shift in the kinds of energy we use. Just as the Greeks and Romans shifted away from slave labor, and the Europeans of the Middle Ages shifted away from wood, the time has come to think up new technologies and learn to use different sources of power.

Nuclear power stations seemed like a great idea at first, but if they leak, radioactive waste destroys both lives and habitats.
DANIËL LEPPENS/DREAMSTIME.COM

ENERGY FACTS: In the eighteenth and nineteenth centuries, one popular fuel was the oil drained from the bodies of dead whales. In fact, whale oil was so popular that some kinds of whales were hunted almost to extinction. So people searched for another energy source and eventually found petroleum (oil).

CHAPTER TWO

What Makes It Go?

The sunflower got its name because its enormous flower turns to face the sun. A bee is sucking nectar from this flower to turn it into honey. Later, that honey could end up on your breakfast toast and power your very next bike ride. BOB ORCHARD

HOW ON EARTH...?

The energy you're using to read this sentence came from the sun.

Okay, okay, most recently it probably came from the cereal you had for breakfast or the sandwich you had for lunch, but the energy in that food came from plants (which grew with energy from the sun) or animals (which ate plants, which grew with energy from the sun). Almost all the energy we can think of comes from the big ball of fire in the sky.

But how can energy travel from the sun, get stored in plants and then be used by humans or car engines or electricity-generating plants? It all has something to do with a chemical called carbon, which can be found just about everywhere on the planet—in every living creature, in the air, in the oceans and in rocks. Carbon is all around us, and it's always on the move, shifting forms, thanks to the sun's energy.

To understand how it works, there's something you need to know: our Earth's got gas. (It's nothing to be embarrassed about, though.) Without those gases, Earth would be too cold to live on, and we wouldn't have any air to breathe. The mixture of gases around the Earth is called the *atmosphere*. The mixture has carbon in it, within a gas called *carbon dioxide*. Carbon dioxide and other gases keep our planet warm. They let sunlight travel

These kids in Benin help grow food for their families. People who grow their own vegetables can watch their gardens turn the sun's energy into supper ingredients. SOLAR ELECTRIC LIGHT FUND

from the sun to Earth's surface and then trap the heat before it escapes back into outer space.

Carbon doesn't hang around in the air forever, though. Plants suck it up and absorb sunlight to make their own food. (We're not talking about plates of lasagna here, of course. Plant food is basically sugar that plants absorb as they grow.) As the plants absorb the food they've made from the carbon in the air, the carbon becomes part of the plant. When the plant dies, other living creatures—from bacteria to people to elephants— might eat it up and use the carbon in their own bodies. They release some of their carbon by breathing out carbon dioxide, which goes into the air, gets sucked up by plants and so on. This carbon cycle has worked as long as there's been life on Earth. That's how things are. Most of the time.

Every tree that we plant sucks some carbon out of the air. And at a time when we've got more carbon in our air than ever before, that's a very exciting thing. FINDHORN FOUNDATION

These squashes were grown for their delicious seeds. Once people have collected the seeds, the vegetable gets tossed into a heap like this one to decompose and become part of the earth again. MICHELLE MULDER

ENERGY FACTS: Even wind energy comes from the sun. The sun heats the air, which makes air rise. Lots of this kind of movement is what causes the wind to blow.

HOW TO MAKE A FOSSIL FUEL

Not all plants get eaten by other creatures. Sometimes, plants die in wet soil. That soil might not have enough oxygen for any living organism to survive. Without living organisms to eat the plant, it—and its carbon—gets trapped. Over hundreds of millions of years, heat and pressure from the Earth's crust compress the plants. The result? The dead plants get smushed into what we call coal, petroleum oil or natural gas (mostly a gas called *methane*).

We call these three substances *fossil fuels*. When we burn them to make our cars run, or to make electricity, we use the energy that those plants stored up when the sun shone on them all those millions of years ago.

With a good amount of wind—clean, free energy—the average sailboat travels at about 9 kilometers per hour (or 5 knots, as they say on the sea). BOB ORCHARD

HOT STUFF!

Picture yourself in the Middle Ages. You need to start a fire. So does everyone else, though, and each time you need firewood, you have to walk farther and farther to find a tree. Then someone shows up with a few lumps of hard black stuff. He calls it the new firewood. You try it. It works, and buying a sack of coal from someone is a lot less work than chopping firewood. What's not to like?

Now fast forward about seven hundred years. You're riding around on your horse. It gets thirsty or hungry, and you have to stop and look for something for it to eat. While you're waiting, one of those newfangled horseless carriages drives by. It gets to its destination a lot faster than you do, and all because it has a big tank full of fuel that keeps the car going fast. Why mess with hungry, thirsty, finicky horses when you can just fill up a gas tank and go?

People had been using fossil fuels for hundreds of years before scientists realized they might have some disadvantages. Every time we burn fossil fuels, we use up oxygen and release other gases into the atmosphere. Sulfur dioxide, nitrogen oxide and nitrogen dioxide rise into the air and dissolve in the water droplets that form clouds, and the water becomes acidic. This acidic water, or acid rain, is unhealthy for plants, and when the acid rain gets into waterways, it hurts fish and water life too.

In many parts of the world, animals continue to be an important way to get things from here to there. MICHELLE MULDER

In many big cities, the air often becomes brown and hazy with smog. If you look on the left side of the Ortoköy Mosque, in Istanbul, Turkey, you'll see the original light color of the stone. The blackened stone in other parts of the building is due to the stone's reaction with smog. BARBARA WATSON

ENERGY FACTS: During the past twenty years, burning fossil fuels has created about three-quarters of human-made carbon dioxide emissions.

This girl in Istanbul, Turkey, is peeking into a common scene. Who needs a clothes dryer when the sun can dry clothes for you? MISHA GITBERG

Power Lines

My friends and I were going camping in the mountains in Peru. We packed warm clothing, several blankets, water, a tent, snacks, and a guinea pig for supper. (They're a common food in this part of the world.) I was very grateful for the donkey that carried our load. At 5,500 meters (18,000 feet) above sea level, it was hard to breathe, and every step was a big effort. It was all worth it, though, for the view, the laughter with friends and the once-in-my-lifetime experience of eating roasted guinea pig brain!

On a camping trip in Peru, our friends brought a donkey to carry our tent and cooking gear.
MICHELLE MULDER

And that's not all. When ancient plants get burned up, the carbon stored in the plants' tissues is released into the atmosphere as carbon dioxide. Other gases, like methane, also escape. These gases are a natural part of the atmosphere, but remember how carbon dioxide and other gases trap the sun's energy to keep Earth warm? For millions of years, the gases have maintained a natural balance, keeping the planet at just the right temperature for all of us to live on it. Now that we're burning fossil fuels, though, we're releasing more of these gases into the atmosphere than ever before. More heat from the sun is getting trapped and can't escape back to outer space. Like a greenhouse, Earth is heating up.

All around the Arctic, climate change is obvious. Summers are longer and warmer than ever before. Ice that used to stay frozen is melting, and water levels are rising. A whole way of life is changing because of it. MICHELLE MULDER

COOL SOLUTIONS

Around the world, people are calling for change. Do we really need to use so much fossil fuel? Aren't there other forms of energy that would be better for the environment?

Many people are coming up with alternatives. Some are sustainable, and some aren't. But all of them are creative, and even when one is a dud, it can spark ideas for other brilliant solutions. Let's see how kids around the world (and their families) get energy from surprising sources.

ENERGY FACTS:
Fossil fuels supply more than 85 percent of our energy.

Passive houses, like this one in Montebello, Québec, are designed to use 90 percent less heating energy than the average building. Solar panels, excellent insulation and other design details make this possible. MALCOLM ISAACS

CHAPTER THREE

Flying on a French Fry!

GROW, GROW, GROW YOUR FUEL

Every time we fill our gas tanks, we pour in fuel that took 500 million years to cook underground. But what if we used plants right away, instead of waiting so many lifetimes for them to turn into fuel?

This was one of the first fuel ideas that inventors had for cars, actually. Mr. Diesel had his peanut-oil idea, and Henry Ford planned to run his Model Ts on ethanol, an alcohol made out of corn. Fuel made from a recently living being is called *biofuel*, and for a while it seemed like a great option. But when people discovered that petroleum oil was cheaper and easier to get, that fuel won the competition.

The team designing the solar-powered plane, Solar Impulse, wants to show that new technologies now make it possible to avoid dependence on fossil fuels.
SOLAR IMPULSE/STÉPHANE GROS

ENERGY FACTS: In 2010, an airplane called Solar Impulse flew for 26 hours on solar energy. The hitch? The plane goes an average of 70 kilometers (44 miles) per hour, about the speed of a car on a city street, and much slower than conventional airplanes. But the team behind Solar Impulse is now building a second, more advanced model, which is intended to fly around the world by 2015, proving that we don't need fossil fuels to fly.

Indonesia was once covered in rain forests, but they're quickly disappearing. Forest fires caused by climate change destroy some. People clearing land to grow palm destroy others. The smoke around this wooden raft comes from a rain forest on fire. GREENPEACE

Not everyone's forgotten about biofuel, though. If your family pulled into a gas station in Brazil, for example, your parents could choose between fuel made from corn and another from sugarcane. In parts of Europe, you could fill the tank with biofuel made from palm oil. How are these fuels made? Scientists use chemical reactions, fermentation (the same process used to make wine or beer) and heat to break down the plants into a liquid that can be used as fuel. It's like a superquick alternative to fossil fuels—the same wholesome plant goodness, without the 500-million-year wait.

But many people object to this kind of fuel too, especially if making biofuel involves burning down trees. In Malaysia and Indonesia, palm growers are burning up millions of acres of tropical forests to clear land for growing palm. All this burning destroys irreplaceable natural habitats and pumps huge amounts of carbon into the atmosphere.

An estimated 40 percent of all the corn grown in the United States goes to making biofuel. Many people disagree with putting food into the gas tank, though.
JASON FOGLER/DREAMSTIME.COM

Another problem with biofuel is that the factories making it are sometimes powered by coal or natural gas. In that case, *making* biofuel might use more fossil fuels than people actually save by using it.

Still others complain that using biofuel can be like tossing food into a gas tank. When companies in Brazil make fuel out of sugarcane, they're using plant matter that was left over *after* the sugar harvest. But when companies make corn biofuel, they grow the corn specifically to make fuel. Is it really right to burn up food as car fuel when we could be feeding hungry people with it instead?

POND SCUM IN YOUR TANK

Now scientists are investigating other crops for biofuel. Picture yourself on a train in India. You look out the window and see small leafy green trees stretching along the rails to the horizon. Did the local people get a crazy deal on decorative shrubs, or do these ones grow naturally, hungry for railway fumes?

The Indian state railway planted millions of jatropha plants along the rails and uses the oil from its seeds to help fuel each train trip. Jatropha can grow in dry places with poor soil, where other plants would never survive, and the seeds are not edible, so it's not like using food for fuel. Airline companies hope to use similar technology to make fuel from jatropha plants, as well as babassu palm seed oil, camelina oilseed and…pond scum.

Yes, pond scum (or algae, as scientists call it) is big news these days. Certain algae produce oils that work as biofuel. Algae grow much faster than other biofuel crops, and since algae can grow in tanks, it doesn't take up much farmland. Some companies are even trying to grow algae in salt water or waste water instead of fresh water. Imagine if every flush of the toilet would help your local algae tank grow more biofuel!

Hundreds of years ago, people looked to rivers to power their activities. Now people are looking at what grows on rivers for power. One day, algae might be a common fuel. IMAGE COURTESY OF CHESAPEAKE BAY PROGRAM

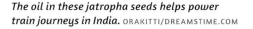

The oil in these jatropha seeds helps power train journeys in India. ORAKITTI/DREAMSTIME.COM

FAST FAST FOOD

While some scientists are poking at plants, others are mucking about with…well…muck. They're looking in their garbage cans and even the sewer system, figuring out how to use what we throw away as an energy source.

What happens, for example, to the oil used to fry French fries at your local fast-food joint? Once it's too dirty to cook with, it usually gets tossed in the garbage or down the drain (even though that's illegal in many places because oil clogs up drains and sewer systems). But did you know that, with a few changes, many cars can run perfectly well on waste vegetable oil?

How? It all goes back to Mr. Diesel in Chapter One, who ran his early engines on peanut oil. Later, he changed them to run on the petroleum mixture named after him. Now that we know how fossil fuels affect the environment, some people with cars that run on diesel are *reversing* the changes that Mr. Diesel made to his engines. These modified engines run perfectly well on the oil that cooked up your French fries, chicken nuggets, tempura or onion rings.

The Big Green Bus is an old Greyhound bus that now runs on waste vegetable oil. Every summer, a dozen or more students from Dartmouth College in New Hampshire make the bus their home, and they travel around the country in it, stopping to talk to people about the environment and how to protect it. They fuel their entire journey with oil that would otherwise have wound up in landfills or gone down the drain. What a way to travel!

This dried-out, mashed-up algae is on its way to becoming biofuel. CELLANA LLC/SERENA CHAMBERLAIN

Kids in Georgia, United States, learn about sustainable fuels from the Big Green Bus team. BIG GREEN BUS

ENERGY FACTS: In 1987, General Motors designed and built a solar-electric vehicle that could race along at about 110 kilometers (68 miles) per hour. The Sunraycer won a 3,000-kilometer (1,900-mile) solar car race across Australia.

THE LITTLE FUNGUS THAT COULD

Don't throw out that orange peel! If people can use waste oil to get around, what about using kitchen scraps? In 2008, scientists at Montana State University told reporters about an exciting tree fungus they'd discovered in Patagonia. What could possibly make a fungus exciting? *Ascocoryne sarcoides* can turn all your plant-based kitchen scraps into a liquid with many of the molecules found in gasoline. (Molecules are parts of matter so tiny that nobody can see them, except with a very special microscope.) Now scientists are working to convince the fungus to make a lot more of this liquid, and perhaps one day, with a bit of help from *A. sarcoides*, we'll be able to leave the fossil fuels in the ground and make car fuel with the wilted lettuce that's in our fridges instead.

THE SCOOP ON POOP

Kitchen garbage isn't the only potential fuel source in your house. For a real stinker of an idea, check out the toilet!

Sweden takes recycling seriously. Only 4 percent of that country's waste winds up in the landfill (compared to almost 66 percent in the United States), and Swedes don't stop at recycling the cartons and apple cores they toss away. They recycle the human waste that gets flushed down the toilet too!

If your family was filling up the gas tank in Stockholm, Sweden, the gas station might have a hose connected directly to—you guessed it—the sewage plant. At the Bromma Wastewater Treatment Plant, machines take the waste that people flush down the toilet, extract and clean the water, and then release the water into the Baltic Sea. That leaves Bromma with over 10 million kilograms (11,000 tons) of solid waste.

Cows are seen as sacred in India, and in some places they wander the streets. Every society has its own idea of what's precious. Will ours one day see garbage as a precious resource?
MISHA GITBERG

It looks like just another lump on a log, but this Ascocoryne sarcoides *fungus can eat up your kitchen scraps and spit out something a lot like gasoline.*
DANIEL SPAKOWICZ

Until the 1970s, that sludge got heaped onto something like a landfill. But then someone thought of a better use for it. First, Bromma used the biogas from the sludge to heat local buildings. Then, in 1994, the treatment plant began processing the sludge to make a high-quality vehicle fuel, and now everyone who poops in Stockholm is helping their neighbors go places, and keeping the Earth cool at the same time!

Recently, Sweden was in the news because the country wants *more* waste. They've used up almost all of theirs, and they need more to power their cities and cars. So they're importing garbage from next-door Norway. What would the world look like if we all treated waste as energy, just waiting to be harvested?

Waste has surprising potential. EERIS TEIPEL

Power Lines

My husband and I moved to Victoria in 2006. The first time we went to a parade here, we got a very good laugh when we spotted someone dancing around dressed as a big piece of poop! For years, James Skwarok put on this costume for all sorts of local events. He wanted to get people talking about the 120 million liters (31 million gallons) of raw sewage that Victoria dumps into the ocean every single day. Thanks in large part to Mr. Floatie and his many supporters, Victoria is now talking about building a brand-new sewage treatment system that will convert solid waste into energy.

Mr. Floatie is a popular local character who showed up in many parades in Victoria, British Columbia, a few years ago.
JAMES SKWAROK

Kites are more than fun. This one is helping a huge ship harness wind energy and reduce its fuel consumption. COPYRIGHT SKYSAILS

ENERGY FACTS: The bicycle is the most energy-efficient vehicle ever invented. The energy you spend pedaling will get you farther than the same energy used by a train, truck or car.

MUSCLE POWER AND ELBOW GREASE

What do we do until *A. sarcoides* turns all our kitchen scraps into biofuel, or everyone has a biogas plant nearby? One of the most sustainable energy sources you can use is…you! Each time you walk somewhere or jump on your bike instead of getting into a car, you're reducing your *carbon footprint*—the amount of carbon your actions release into the atmosphere—and you're getting a good workout too.

Riding bicycles and walking are good for the environment, good for our health and even good for people's wallets. Studies show that when more people ride bicycles, governments save money on both road repair and health care. That's why, in many places, governments ensure that pedaling and walking are safe, easy and fun.

In the Netherlands, 30 to 40 percent of all trips are made by bicycle, and this bicycle parking area in Maastricht, Netherlands, isn't at all unusual. MICHELLE MULDER

In some parts of the world, almost everyone owns a car. In other parts of the world, people use other ways to get around. Check out the variety of transportation options in this intersection in Marrakech, Morocco. MICHELLE MULDER

Power Lines

Where I live, just about everything we need is within walking distance. When we want to get somewhere fast, we ride our bicycles. And if we really need a car, we borrow one from the Car Share Co-op, an organization that has several cars parked in different places in the city for people to borrow. We like cycling because it's great exercise, it gets us out into the community and parking is easy. We also save money because we don't need a car, car insurance, gasoline or a gym membership!

My family loves cycling. In rainy weather, my daughter stays warm and dry, riding in the front of our box-bike.
GASTÓN CASTAÑO

CHAPTER FOUR

Flicking the Switch

HAVE A POWERFUL DAY

What did you do when you woke up this morning? Did you squint at the numbers on the alarm clock, flick on the light and then take a hot shower? In most of North America, electricity keeps our houses warm (or cool) and bright. It preserves our food, lets us listen to music at the touch of a button and even connects us to billions of other people through the Internet. But almost a quarter of the world's population doesn't have access to electricity. And those of us who do are rethinking how we get it. Most North American power plants use fossil fuels to generate electricity. But if we're learning how to replace fossil fuels to get around, surely we can think up other ways to get electricity, right?

Absolutely! Around the world, people are already powering their daily activities in many creative ways.

PLOP! SIZZLE!

What if you need to build a fire, and you don't have wood or coal (or lighter fluid, for that matter)?

People have been using sundried animal poop as fuel for thousands of years. In some places in India, children spend part

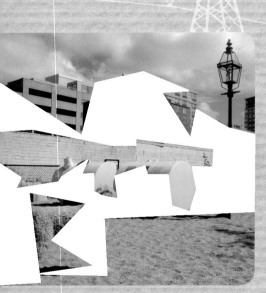

In Cambridge, Massachusetts, Matthew Mazzotta has set up the Park Spark Project, a public art project where people can drop their dog's doo into a digester that sucks out the energy in the poop and uses it to light up the park.
MATTHEW MAZZOTTA/PARKSPARKPROJECT.COM

Kids at Kasiisi Primary School in Uganda watch the construction of the biogas digester at their school. This biodigester will run mostly on human bodily waste, but to get started, it needed to be primed with 8,000 kg (8.8 tons) of cow manure. Kids brought it all from home in bag after bag after bag. Now that's teamwork! GREEN HEAT UGANDA LTD. / VIANNEY TUMWESIGE

This solar cooker in Ladakh, India, concentrates the sun's heat on the kettle in the middle. Why burn fuel when the sun can boil water for you? FALK66/DREAMSTIME.COM

of every day patting animal dung into little bricks that dry in the sun. Dried poop burns well, animals are always making more of it and it's free. When your family has barely enough money to survive, free fuel means you get to eat.

But burning poop is dangerous. Every poop fire releases carbon-filled smoke. That smoke gets into people's eyes and lungs and can cause diseases like cancer.

In China, five million families use their poop in another way: they digest it! But wait. It's not as gross as it sounds. Their toilets and their pigsties are connected to underground chambers called *biodigesters*. There, the waste breaks down into a sludge that can be safely used for fertilizer and a gas that can be used as a smoke-free cooking fuel. Using human and animal waste for fuel also means people don't chop down as many trees to build cooking fires. Local forests can continue to pull greenhouse gases out of the air, keeping the entire planet happier.

Solar panels allow these young women in Benin to bring water to their gardens and grow more produce than ever before. Having more food to sell at the market means having money for things like school fees and medical treatment. SOLAR ELECTRIC LIGHT FUND

BRIGHT IDEAS

Have you ever seen a calculator with a small gray panel at the top? That panel is a *photovoltaic cell*, and the materials inside produce an electric current when light shines on them. Many homes around the world use the same technology. On yurts in Mongolia and rowhouses in Germany, PV cells—or solar panels—use the sun's energy to power everything from TVs to microwaves to laptops.

With this technology, you'd think that sunny places like parts of Africa or the Caribbean would be making so much electricity that they could sell it to cloudier places. But solar panels are expensive, and plenty of people in sunny places can't afford them. That's why organizations like Solar Electric Light Fund (SELF) raise money to buy solar technology for villagers in developing countries. Solar panels can help villagers pump and filter water, establish medical clinics, light up communities to increase safety and power schools.

Solar panels can run lights, medical equipment, computers, irrigation systems and many other things that will make a world of difference to the lives of these kids in Benin.
SOLAR ELECTRIC LIGHT FUND

BANANAS ON ICE

Did you know that Icelanders grow their own bananas? How? Don't look up at the sun this time. Look down. Deep in the Earth's core is a layer of gases and rock so hot that it's melted into a liquid called *magma*. When a volcano erupts, that liquid rock comes bursting out of the ground. But that's not the only way that the Earth's internal heat can escape. Sometimes it comes to the surface as hot springs—water that comes out of the ground piping hot. Hot springs are the reason bananas can grow in Iceland. The country has so many hot springs that it heats its buildings with them.

This heat energy from inside the Earth is called *geothermal energy*, and the supply is practically limitless. Of course, in most of the world, we don't find hot springs around every corner.

We get our English word geyser *from Geysir, a shooting hot spring in Iceland. When it erupts, Geysir shoots boiling water up to 70 m (230 ft) into the air. Now that's power!*
MERLIN BACKUS AND REBECCA VELAZQUEZ

If you get hungry at Hveragerði's geothermal park in Iceland, you can buy an egg and cook it in a nearby stream. MERLIN BACKUS AND REBECCA VELAZQUEZ

But in Japan, the Philippines, the west coast of South America and parts of the United States (like California), magma is closer to the surface than in other parts of the world—close enough for people to reach the heat by drilling deep. Send water down those holes, and it rises up again as steam. This steam can turn turbines to generate electricity.

One problem with geothermal energy is that it may give off chemicals known as sulfur compounds. These stink and make rain acidic, which destroys forests and damages buildings. Engineers are working on ways to filter out sulfur gases, though. Researchers from the Massachusetts Institute of Technology believe that geothermal energy could supply 20,000 times as much as the United States needs every year!

HANG ON TO YOUR HAT

Has the wind ever blown a hat off your head? What if the energy from that wind could light up your home and keep your computer running?

That's the way things work in Samsø, a small island in Denmark. Over 4,000 people live there, and until 1997, all their energy came from coal and oil they imported from the mainland. Then, in the mid-1990s, the Danish government challenged communities across the country to switch to renewable resources. The people of Samsø built ten wind turbines offshore, and by 2006 they didn't need fossil fuels anymore. Every last zap of electricity came from their turbines.

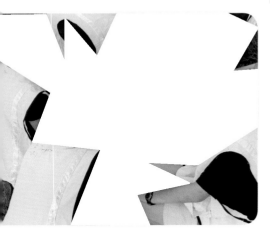

Students at a school in Idaho enjoy learning how to construct a wind turbine. The Wind for Schools program in the United States installs small wind turbines at schools, both to provide sustainable energy and to teach communities about the power of wind. WIND FOR SCHOOLS PROJECT/BILLIE JOHNSON

ENERGY FACTS: Half the world's population uses 95 percent of the world's energy resources. And nearly all of those resources are fossil fuels.

In recent years, people have built turbines all over the world. Some people love them. Other people say they're ugly and use more fossil fuels than they save: for electricity to be available, the turbines have to keep spinning, and if they stop, machines keep them going, usually by burning fossil fuels. Not every place is perfect for a wind turbine, but it doesn't mean that wind turbines are a bad idea everywhere. Like solar energy and geothermal energy, in the right situation, wind energy could really blow your socks off.

WAVE AND SMILE

What's that wiggly thing out in the water? A shark? A sea monster? Or…a wave-energy converter?

The Pelamis is a long red-and-yellow tube that floats on the water near the Island of Hoy in Orkney, Scotland. Every time ocean waves pass the tube, it bends, and motors inside convert the movement to electrical power. This technology—named for a sea snake that it resembles—is part of a test project. By 2015, the Pelamis Wave Technology company wants to know enough about harnessing wave energy to be able to export its technology around the world.

Waves, rivers and waterfalls can all generate electricity; the movement of falling water—instead of the burning of fossil fuels—generates electrical power. Hydro power plants aren't perfect for every watery location, though. Building huge dams can devastate a landscape. For example, the Three Gorges dam in China flooded so much land that 1.2 million people had to move away from their homes. We can only guess how many plants and animals were displaced or died. But in the right spot, and with the right technology, the energy of water movement could power homes for years to come. Like wind, solar power and biofuels, it's all a question of choosing the best power source for the time and place.

When Pelamis rides the waves, a motor inside converts the movement to electrical energy that is sent back to shore through underwater cables. Ride on! PELAMIS WAVE POWER

In hydroelectric dams, falling water turns turbines that are connected to generators. The generators convert the movement of the turbines to electricity, which lights up and heats houses, farms, office buildings and factories. SAMOTREBIZAN/DREAMSTIME.COM

These kids are lighting up their lives by playing soccer in Guadalajara, Mexico.
UNCHARTED PLAY

THE POWER OF PLAY

In some parts of the world, playing soccer is now an important family chore, thanks to a new invention by four Harvard students. Their creation is sOccket: a soccer ball with a machine inside that captures the movement energy of a rolling ball. This energy charges a battery inside the ball, and this battery can then power a lamp. Thirty minutes of play creates enough power for three hours of light. And if a few minutes of play can light up a room, maybe one day kids on the playground will be powering entire schools!

MEANWHILE, IN THE LIVING ROOM...

One day, maybe every household will have a sOccket or solar panels, or we'll all be connected to biofuel plants. In the meantime, though, what can we do about the fossil fuels affecting our planet?

Kids and adults around the world are coming up with creative ways to use less fuel. For example, in the slums of Manila, Philippines, people live in tiny shacks made from sheets of metal. Until recently, the shacks were completely dark inside. Anyone who was too old or sick to go outside had to spend every day in darkness. But one day, Illac Diaz, who is part of an organization called My Shelter Foundation, looked at an empty pop bottle and had an idea. Soon, all around the slum, people were cutting small bottle-sized holes into the roofs, inserting a pop bottle (with a few teaspoons of bleach inside to keep dangerous molds from growing) and gluing the bottle into the roof. Suddenly, light poured down into places where people had never had light before.

What do you get when you mix plastic bottles, bleach, water and glue with a good dose of creative thinking? Light in more than 15,000 homes in the Philippines! This brilliant idea is fast spreading to other countries, such as Peru and Colombia. MY SHELTER FOUNDATION

Kelvin Doe is the 2012 winner of the Global Minimum Innovate Salone competition, in Sierra Leone. When Kelvin was thirteen, he built batteries with spare parts from the trash near his home and used the batteries to power his very own radio station. That radio station allowed people to solve problems together. Kelvin's creative thinking turned trash into an important community resource. GLOBAL MINIMUM INC.

This computer at a school in Peru runs on power from a micro-hydro system.
GREEN EMPOWERMENT/ANNA GARWOOD

Creative ideas like this are changing the world. And although your parents probably wouldn't appreciate you putting pop-bottle skylights into your own ceiling, you can do plenty of other things to save fuel.

Use human power

Bike or walk whenever you can. And use your own inner human heater instead of cranking up the thermostat. Pulling on a sweater can reduce your carbon footprint.

Use what you've got

Redesign clothes that you're bored with or that don't fit anymore. Feast on leftovers. Save seeds from your favorite veggies and grow a garden. Toss kitchen scraps into the compost. Every time you reuse something or recycle it, you're saving the fuel that would be spent on making something new and transporting it to stores.

Use a superpower—consumer power!

Did you know that every time you choose long-lasting products without much packaging you're saving fuel? No one will have to haul away a package or broken bits, and you won't have to buy a replacement. The decisions we make at a store can have a very big impact on the world around us.

ZOOMING AHEAD

Way back in Chapter One, we saw how people changed energy sources every time one ran out. When the Romans ran out of slaves, they began to develop water technology. When whales were hunted almost to extinction, people used petroleum (oil) instead. Each new discovery and change led to more discoveries.

ENERGY FACTS:
In Oslo, Norway, heat from the city's sewers is piped around underground to keep 9,000 apartments warm.

Right now we're at another one of those exciting turning points. The overuse of fossil fuels is damaging our environment, and it's time to use different kinds of energy. So far, no one's come up with a single perfect sustainable fuel that will work everywhere for all people, but who says we need to? Not everyone eats the same food or speaks the same language. Not all landscapes are the same. And not all power sources need to be the same either.

Every day people are coming up with creative ways to both save energy and draw on what we've got to meet our needs: biofuel, solar power, geothermal, wind, waste energy, wave energy and human power. It's all right here, waiting to be used. And who knows what the next big discovery might be!

Power Lines

Electricity is expensive in Bolivia, and people use it far less than we do in Canada. For example, when my husband and I traveled there, we slept with lots and lots of blankets because there was no electric heat. In Potosí, Bolivia, I counted eleven wool blankets on the beds. In Villazón, each bed had so many heavy blankets that the person underneath sank right into the mattress, leaving a flat surface on top. When I went back to our tiny room one evening, I couldn't find my husband anywhere until he stuck his hand out from under the bedding and called, "I'm here!"

Isla del Sol (Island of the Sun) is a small island in Bolivia. It has no paved roads and no vehicle traffic. As in many parts of Bolivia, most people do not have electricity. They rely on other power sources to get things done. GASTÓN CASTAÑO

Resources

Books

Challoner, Jack. *Energy.* New York, NY: DK Children, 2000.
Drummond, Allan. *Energy Island: How One Community Harnessed the Wind and Changed Their World.* New York, NY: Farrar, Straus and Giroux, 2011.
Kelsey, Elin. *Not Your Typical Book about the Environment.* Toronto, ON: Owlkids, 2010.

Websites

Alliant Energy Kids: http://www.alliantenergykids.com/
The Big Green Bus: Vehicle for Change: http://www.thebiggreenbus.org/
The Global Hope Network—Solar Cooking: http://solarcooking.wikia.com/
Green Heat Uganda: http://greenheatug.wordpress.com
Liter of Light: http://aliteroflight.org
The Park Spark Project: http://parksparkproject.com/
Pelamis Wave Power: http://www.pelamiswave.com
sOccket: http://unchartedplay.com
Solar Electric Light Fund: http://self.org

Acknowledgments

If someone had told me in school that I'd one day write a science book, I would have laughed. *Brilliant!* exists because of the passion and generosity of people around the world who taught me what I needed to know. I'd like to say a big thank-you to each of them, so grab a snack, rev up your reading engine and hold on.

Thanks to all my friends who listened and offered suggestions while I sorted out what I wanted to say, especially Susan Braley, Binnie Brennan, Julie Brown, Gastón Castaño and Mark Weston. I'm very grateful to Maureen Parker—godmother, friend and photographer extraordinaire—for enthusiastically calling out for photographs for this book. Thank you to the Sidney Shutterbugs for answering that call.

I'm grateful for Tamara Dean's book *The Human-Powered Home: Choosing Muscles Over Motors* for helping me understand the ways humans have used energy resources over the millennia. Thank you to Daniel Spakowicz for helping me see what fungus has to do with fuel.

For spectacular images, contacts and information from around the world, I send heartfelt thanks to Ali Paul, Karen Poggi, David Cantrell, Chris Lumens, Sandy Cardon, Maya Viavant and Joanna Schneider, Alenka Zibetto, Sarah Poirier, Deborah Smith, Malcolm Isaacs, Margo McLoughlin, Misha Gitberg, Sherri Phillips, Carin Bolles, John Alejandro, Serena Chamberlain, the volunteers at Greenpeace, Margaret Enloe, Daniel Spakowicz, Vianney Tumwesige, Alison Dalton Smith, Bob Orchard, Barbara Watson, Ken Rothe, Mark Weston,

David Moinina Sengeh, Eeris Teipel, Henry Mulder, Melanie Fricot, Matthew Mazzotta, Brandon Leudke, James Skwarok, Grace Magney, Diaz Illac Angelo, and Merlin and Rebecca (whose awesome travel blog gave me a free tour of Europe!).

Thanks to HOPE International for bringing me to the Dominican Republic in 1996, my teammates, and the people of El Higuito who taught me so much. I'm also thankful to Melanie Fricot, Rosa Villón and the people of Pamparomas, Peru, who showed me that happiness depends on the sustained energy of love and laughter.

I am grateful to Orca Book Publishers for the opportunity to write this book. Many thanks to Sarah Harvey for her guidance and insightful editing, and to Teresa Bubela and Jenn Playford for their patience and beautiful book design.

I especially want to thank all the members of my family who listened to me spout sustainable energy facts for months and didn't groan or roll their eyes even once. Now that's love.

Thank you, everyone.

If waste vegetable oil can get the Big Green Bus around the United States every summer, who knows where our creative thinking will take us next! BIG GREEN BUS

Index

Page numbers in **bold** indicate an image; there may also be text related to the same topic on that page

Index (continued)